To Esther
May God g[ive you]
a most Wonderful trip.

Bernie

Portrait of Antarctica

Jim Bishop
Launcelot Fleming
Paul Goodall-Copestake
Jonathan Walton
Kevin Walton

Foreword by HRH The Prince of Wales

PORTRAIT OF
ANTARCTICA

George Philip

British Library Cataloguing in Publication Data

Portrait of Antarctica.
   1. Antarctic regions – Discovery and exploration
   – Pictorial works
   I. Walton, K.
   919.8′904   G860

ISBN 0 540 01075 8

© Kevin Walton 1983
Published by George Philip, 12–14 Long Acre, London
WC2E 9LP

Reprinted 1984

Printed in Hong Kong

TITLE PAGE *Travelling long distances with skidoos can
be very lonely. For safety's sake in crevassed areas a
very long tow-rope is used with one man on the skidoo
and one on the sledge. At this lunchtime halt in
George VI Sound the skidoo apparently has no driver:
he took the picture. It is early spring 1975 and the low
midday sun is lighting up the sedimentary rocks where
fossils were first found in 1936.*

Acknowledgements
Our thanks are due to the following who have helped us in
producing this book: to the Trustees of the Scott Polar
Research Institute and expedition members, who have
allowed us to use the BGLE photographs in their
copyright; to Richard Otto, Dave Burkitt and the British
Antarctic Survey who each contributed a photograph; to
Ann Todd of the British Antarctic Survey who searched
out original negatives for us; to NASA for the Landsat
photograph on p. 29; to the US Geological Survey for
supplying us with the aerial photograph on p. 32; to Lester
Goodall-Copestake for taking on the job of producing the
chapter on Wildlife from his son Paul's letters and
photographs; to Peter Prince for reading the Wildlife
chapter for us; to Jane Bishop for encouraging us to use
the photographs taken by her late husband; to Lydia
Greeves of George Philip for the tactful and kindly way in
which she handled the difficult job of reconciling her role
as editor with the demands of sometimes incoherent polar
enthusiasts; above all to Ruth Walton who accepted the
disruption that writing a book of this sort creates and
produced readable manuscript out of illegible chaos.
Finally, it has been a great honour for us that HRH The
Prince of Wales has contributed such a personal and
generous foreword.

Contents

Antarctic fur seals crowd the beaches of tiny Bird Island, where over 30,000 seal pups were born the year before. (1983)

BUCKINGHAM PALACE

Antarctica is so far away from our daily lives, so unlikely ever to impinge on our existence, that most of us are unconcerned that we know very little about this ice-covered continent which is bigger than China and India and yet where, in any given winter, only 2000 people live, of whom only 2 or 3 are women.

The history of Man's activities on this continent is less than a hundred years old: this book concentrates on a representative chunk of over half that period, from the 1930s to the 1980s, largely as seen through the eyes of five members of British scientific bodies, four of whom happen to be related to each other. What they saw and photographed in the deep South, during various periods between 1934 and 1982, has been condensed here to produce an interesting and accurate glimpse of what life is like in Antarctica for the people who work there.

The evolution over fifty years of rough huts into fairly sophisticated bases is graphically depicted through the excellent selection of photographs; monochromes for the earlier scenes and magnificent colour for the 70s and 80s.

The attitude to life of the many individuals who have manned these remote bases year after year is clearly one of self-reliance and optimism, despite often difficult circumstances and unforeseen setbacks.

As well as providing an attractive collection of photographs of scenery and wildlife in a continent as yet unspoilt by man and still holding many secrets from him, this book manages to get across what it is like actually to live and work there from day to day and the way conditions have changed since the pioneering days of the early twentieth century.

I have nothing but the greatest admiration for the kind of adventuring spirit which prompts men to explore this vast and unforgiving territory. It is clear from the way in which this book has been compiled (I found it spellbinding) and from the concise, often humorous, comments it contains that those who come to know the Antarctic are enriched and humbled by the experience. And how important it is for our general sanity to be made to feel small by the grandeur and elemental power of Mother Nature! If we can't reach Antarctica, at least we can be enthralled by its spell through the observations of others.

Charles .

To the many friends we would never have made but for the Antarctic.

Introduction

The last fifty years have been a key period in the history of Antarctica during which there have been many significant and far-reaching changes. Although South Georgia was discovered by Captain Cook in 1775 the Antarctic Continent was not sighted until 1820 and, over a century later, when the first photographs in this collection were taken, it was still only the fringes that had been seen by man. The maps showing the South Polar region and the Antarctic Peninsula as known in 1933 and as known today demonstrate only too clearly how much has been achieved in the intervening years. Apart from the major advances in our knowledge of the continent, these decades also mark the end of the heroic era of exploration, typified by the expeditions of Scott and Shackleton, and the start of a new era in which expeditions are primarily concerned with scientific research of one kind or another.

The underlying purpose of all exploration is to extend our knowledge and understanding of the world but in the early years, for obvious reasons, exploration in the sense of discovery took priority over everything else. But once maps were available and time and money allowed, fieldwork has been directed towards research with very different ends. Ground projects include measuring the thickness of the ice cover and the nature and shape of the rocks underneath, while the isolation of the continent and its nearness to the Pole makes it an ideal platform for research concerned with the weather, the atmosphere and electrical phenomena in the ionosphere above. For work of this latter kind, scientists live in large, permanently-manned bases and travelling is seldom necessary. On the Antarctic islands, such as South Georgia and Bird Island, all-the-year-round studies are possible observing the wildlife that depends on the rich southern oceans.

Just as the purpose of exploration in the Antarctic has changed, so have the equipment and means of communication available. The period covered here starts when huskies were still the main form of transport and when parties in the field were truly on their own. It ends when mechanical vehicles have taken over completely, when radio is used to keep in touch with isolated groups and when aids to navigation include satellite photographs showing surface conditions over a wide area.

This book is a portrait of a continent in transition as seen through the eyes of five men who have lived and worked there over the last fifty years. Many of the earliest photographs were taken by Launcelot Fleming on the British Graham Land Expedition (BGLE) during 1934–7. This small, privately-funded expedition, led by the Australian John Rymill, was the second to go south with the plan to overwinter on the west side of the Antarctic Peninsula. The main aim of the expedition was survey, for very little was known about the area and what was known of the southernmost part was largely based on the single flight of Sir Hubert Wilkins a few years earlier.

In 1945, under the British Colonial Office, expeditions were given official status as the Falkland Islands Dependencies Survey (FIDS), which consolidated and extended the work of the BGLE on the Antarctic Peninsula over the period 1945–8. Kevin Walton, who took the photographs dating from this period, was part of a team that built and worked from a new base within

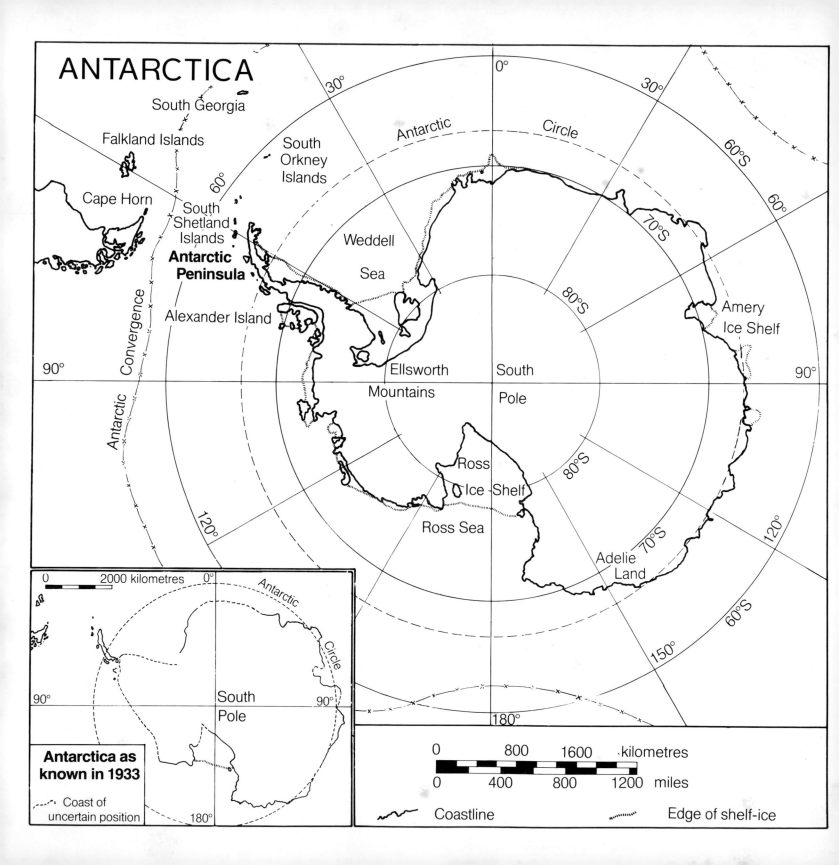

ANTARCTICA

South Georgia

Falkland Islands

Cape Horn

South Orkney Islands

0°

30°

30°

60°S

60°

60°

70°S

80°S

90°

South Shetland Islands

Antarctic Peninsula

Alexander Island

Weddell Sea

Antarctic Circle

Amery Ice Shelf

90°

Convergence

Antarctic

Ellsworth Mountains

South Pole

Ross Ice Shelf

Ross Sea

Adelie Land

120°

80°S

70°S

120°

150°

60°S

180°

0 2000 kilometres

0°

Antarctic

90°

Circle

90°

South Pole

180°

Antarctica as known in 1933

- - - - Coast of uncertain position

0   800   1600   kilometres

0   400   800   1200   miles

Coastline   Edge of shelf-ice

the Antarctic Circle. During the period 1946–7 the privately-organized American Ronne Antarctic Research Expedition had its base only about 200 metres away from this FIDS base. Kevin Walton was also involved in the South Georgia Survey of 1950–1, a privately-run expedition to the incompletely mapped island of South Georgia.

In 1962 the FIDS was reorganized as the British Antarctic Survey (BAS), which now maintains a series of permanent bases in Antarctica extending from the southern end of the Weddell Sea to Bird Island, South Georgia. These bases are manned by small overwintering

In 1947 the sea-ice in Marguerite Bay was very slow to clear and this was typical of the conditions the relief-ship John Biscoe *faced on the way out. The sun is setting but will be up again in two or three hours. In full daylight this pack-ice did not present many problems.*

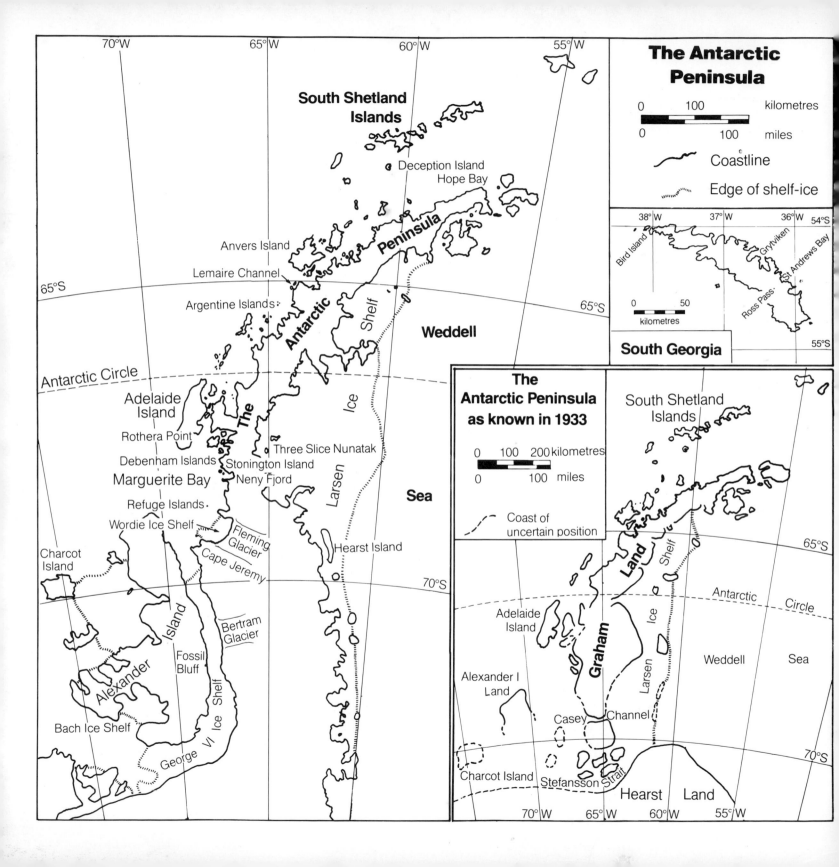

The Antarctic Peninsula

0   100   kilometres
0   100   miles

⌒ Coastline
⌒⌒⌒ Edge of shelf-ice

70°W   65°W   60°W   55°W

**South Shetland
Islands**

Deception Island
Hope Bay

Anvers Island

Lemaire Channel

Argentine Islands

65°S

Antarctic

Peninsula

Ice

Shelf

Weddell

65°S

Antarctic Circle

Adelaide
Island

Rothera Point

Debenham Islands

Marguerite Bay

The

Three Slice Nunatak

Stonington Island
Neny Fjord

Larsen

Sea

Refuge Islands

Wordie Ice Shelf

Fleming
Glacier

Cape Jeremy

Charcot
Island

Island

Bertram
Glacier

Fossil
Bluff

Hearst Island

70°S

Alexander

Bach Ice Shelf

George VI Ice Shelf

South Georgia

38°W   37°W   36°W   54°S

Bird Island

Grytviken

St Andrews Bay

Ross Pass.

0   50
kilometres

55°S

The
Antarctic Peninsula
as known in 1933

0   100   200 kilometres
0   100   miles

⌒ Coast of
uncertain position

South Shetland
Islands

65°S

Antarctic   Circle

Adelaide
Island

Graham   Land

Larsen

Ice

Shelf

Weddell   Sea

Alexander I
Land

Casey   Channel

70°S

Charcot Island

Stefansson Strait

Hearst   Land

70°W   65°W   60°W   55°W

groups which are joined by large summer parties for fieldwork in the daylight months.

Jim Bishop went south in 1972–5 as part of a BAS team at their small advance base at Fossil Bluff, directly beneath the mountain of the same name where Launcelot Fleming had found fossils in 1936. Jonathan Walton joined him to work at Fossil Bluff during 1973–6 and Jonathan went south again for a season in 1978. Most of the work at this base was concerned with glaciology as there is access from the base to glaciers of all sizes and speeds as well as to a large ice shelf.

Most of the wildlife photographs were taken by Paul Goodall-Copestake while he was working for BAS at its most northerly bases on South Georgia and Bird Island. These bases are manned by small teams and are important centres for the study of Antarctic wildlife. Apart from a brief period in 1982 when work was interrupted by the Falklands dispute, Paul has been there since 1980.

The photographs taken by these five men vividly portray the everyday experience of living and working in Antarctica, sometimes under difficult and daunting conditions. The image of the continent they present includes the kind of detail that only comes from long, first-hand experience – a true *Portrait of Antarctica*.

Biographical Notes

Launcelot Fleming was chaplain and geologist of the British Graham Land Expedition 1934–7. He was a naval chaplain throughout World War II, and Dean of Trinity Hall immediately before and after the war. He has been Bishop of Portsmouth, Bishop of Norwich and Dean of Windsor. He was a member of the initiating committee for the Duke of Edinburgh Award Scheme, helped to found Voluntary Service Overseas and is a trustee of the Prince's Trust. He is Knight Commander of the Victorian Order and holder of the Polar Medal.

Kevin Walton is a professional civil engineer who served with the Falkland Islands Dependencies Survey in 1945–8 and was second-in-command of the South Georgia Survey 1950–1. He has been an Outward Bound instructor and a civilian lecturer at RN College, Dartmouth. He is now involved in recruitment in schools for professional engineering. He holds the George Cross, the DSC and the Polar Medal and is author of *Two Years in the Antarctic*.

Jonathan Walton, Kevin Walton's son, is a graduate civil engineer who worked as a surveyor/glaciologist with BAS in 1973–6, latterly as base leader at Fossil Bluff. In 1978 he returned to Antarctica for a season. He is currently teaching and was chief surveyor of the International Karakoram Project, 1980.

Jim Bishop was an engineer and worked as a surveyor and glaciologist with BAS in 1972–5, ultimately as base leader at Fossil Bluff. Married to Jonathan Walton's sister Jane, he was tragically killed on the International Karakoram Project, 1980.

Paul Goodall-Copestake, Kevin Walton's nephew, is a zoologist and ornithologist who joined BAS as a biological assistant in 1980. He is currently working with BAS on Bird Island, South Georgia, where his primary concern is the study of fur seals and albatrosses.

The Hostile Land

THE ANTARCTIC CONTINENT is the last great wilderness – equivalent in area to the United States and Central America as far as Panama, all but $4\frac{1}{2}$ per cent of this vast area is permanently ice-covered. It is the highest land-mass in the world, with an average height over 2000 metres, and it is also the continent with the lowest surface temperatures. About 90 per cent of the world's ice is locked up here, in places reaching depths of 4000 metres. If all this ice were to melt the world's sea-level would rise by about 80 metres. Nelson could step off his column into a boat, the Statue of Liberty would be submerged and most of the Netherlands and Denmark would be under water.

Antarctica is often said to resemble a gigantic iced cake, with its ice-sheet 'icing' gradually spreading outwards and flowing over the edge. But this analogy ignores the fact that the icing is covering a cake of dubious quality. The ice-sheet is often much thicker than the cake it covers and in many areas there is no cake at all, for the land-mass supporting it is well below sea-level. With the ice cover stripped off, Antarctica would appear as a mountainous continent about three-quarters of its present size and with an average height similar to that of Australia. At the edges of the continent the polar ice forms floating shelf-ice, many hundreds of metres thick, from which enormous icebergs break away and move slowly northwards, disintegrating as they go.

The continent is not only the coldest but also the windiest place on earth. Temperatures of $-80°C$ have been recorded on the central plateau and the cold air masses that form here move outwards and downwards like water off an upturned plate and build up into winds of incredible ferocity on their way to the coast. It is windy everywhere, but Adelie Land, with a full gale for two hundred days a year, lays claim to being the windiest

PREVIOUS PAGE *A typical Antarctic panorama. The cliff on the right marks the edge of the peninsular plateau and falls 1000 metres to the glacier below. The dark line across the frozen sea in the distance is the shadow of the only cloud in the sky. (1975)*

place on earth. The cold air masses freeze the sea surface in winter to form continuous sheets of ice extending hundreds of miles from the shore.

Although Antarctica is covered by an enormous accumulation of ice and snow, actual annual snowfall on the continent is not very great. Over the central plateau it is rarely more than 60 millimetres of water equivalent a year but at the fringes, particularly near the areas of exposed rock and on the offshore islands, it can reach 1.5 metres. Although snowfall is slight, snow never disappears. It will be blown around by the polar winds and under the influence of the sun and increasing pressure from fresh snowfalls it will gradually become part of the ice-sheet that covers the continent and start a relentless journey to the sea that may take hundreds or thousands of years.

Antarctica lies almost entirely within the Polar Circle but the influence of the great ice-sheet reaches much further. The polar climate extends as far as the line known as the Antarctic Convergence, where there is a marked change to milder temperatures. Several groups of islands, including South Georgia, the South Orkneys and the South Shetlands, lie within the line of the Convergence and are always considered part of Antarctica.

The Antarctic Peninsula and its offshore islands, where most of these photographs were taken, is an extension of the Andes. It is a high, snow-covered tongue reaching to within 900 miles of Cape Horn. Here winds blowing outwards from the Pole are locally distorted to give fierce gales funnelling down the narrow glaciers flowing off the Peninsula's central plateau. Off the west coast of the Peninsula lies Alexander Island, the only large proven island of the continent, separated from the mainland by a wide channel covered with shelf-ice. Further south, where the Peninsula joins the rest of Antarctica, the Ellsworth Mountains rise straight out of the shelf-ice to heights of over 5100 metres. These are the highest mountains on the continent and include some of the greatest rock faces in the world.

Antarctica is a land of distant views and great beauty, a land unspoiled and free from man-made artefacts. This chapter is about its varied landscapes, its moods and contrasts. An almost uncanny peace and stillness at one moment can give way to roaring blizzards the next, while the restless continuity of daylight in summer turns to unrelieved darkness in winter. It is a lonely land but not by any stretch of the imagination is it dull – Antarctica presents formidable problems and considerable dangers but such challenges are fascinating and the rewards in meeting them considerable.

Fine-weather aerial views in the Antarctic are stupendous and only from the air can the sheer size of this land be appreciated. There are many areas as yet unvisited by man and it is a climber's paradise – 98 per cent of the peaks are still unclimbed. (1979)

ABOVE RIGHT *When great masses of moving ice meet unyielding rock the ice has to give way, forming enormous pressure ridges. The scale is difficult to judge but the diminutive figure gives the game away.* (1975)

RIGHT *Spectacular ice-falls spill over the edges of the plateau of the Antarctic Peninsula. The drop involved here is about 1500 metres – needless to say, this is not one of the recommended routes to or from the plateau. (1974)*

Where the polar ice-sheet meets the sea the ice may float and form shelf-ice. This is the Bach Ice Shelf, showing the ice front where the ice breaks off to form enormous flat-topped icebergs which may be several miles long. Some of the ice in the distance will have come from the shelf but some will be last winter's thin sea-ice which is gradually breaking up and melting. (1974)

This aerial picture of a glacier snout shows a heavily-crevassed glacier reaching the sea. It is about a mile from one side to the other. (1974)

It is early spring and the winter ice between the Argentine Islands and the mainland is obviously on the move (note the rough edges to the floes). In winter sea-ice is most treacherous – it appears smooth and solid but high winds will break it up and take it out to sea in hours. (1935)

Ice from the distant peaks slowly flows downhill ending up as enormous chunks breaking off the snout of a glacier like the one shown here. The ice cliffs in the foreground are about 30 metres high and even in the winter when the sea is frozen it would be impossible to scale them and reach the surface of the glacier. (1974)

The Lemaire Channel is the standard route for ships proceeding to bases further south, although the precipitous cliffs either side are higher than the channel is wide (about 900 metres). (1975)

*These enormous, jumbled blocks of ice tower some
20 metres or so and would make overland progress
both difficult and dangerous. In the distance the
mountains of Alexander Island are impressive even
though they are 70 miles away. (1974)*

This inhospitable coast is typical of conditions on the west of the Peninsula. The 2000-metre rock buttress (one-and-a-half times as high as the north face of the Eiger) separates small hanging glaciers from which the icebergs in the foreground have calved – they will probably last another year or so before disintegrating. (1974)

Winter over George VI Ice Shelf. The smooth ice in the foreground is 'fast ice', rigidly attached to the rock. The obvious line is the tide crack – on the seaward side the floating shelf-ice will move up and down with the tide by as much as two metres. (1974)

A typical glacier flowing gently from the peninsular plateau down to the sea. It is about two miles wide and nineteen miles long and although it's heavily crevassed in places it would probably be possible to find a route up on to the plateau. (1974)

Where the Fleming Glacier starts floating, to become the Wordie Ice Shelf, the 'hinge zone' is particularly chaotic. This view from the air shows great sweeping curves of wide crevasses interspersed with 'crazy paving' over sub-ice obstructions. Frequent and violent katabatic winds have formed the drift patterns that in places fill the 30-metre deep chasms. (1974)

RIGHT The extent of the snow cover in Antarctica is shown very clearly on satellite pictures. This photograph was taken from a height of about 620 miles and covers an area about 90 miles square. The details of the crevassing show up well. (1979)

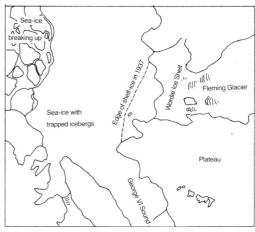

Broken sea-ice off the coast of the
Antarctic Peninsula. The small
ice-floes provide ideal sunbathing
sites for seals and other wildlife.
In the distance are the Lemaire
Channel and the mountains leading
up to the peninsular plateau. (1976)

ABOVE *On the plateau vast stretches of gently undulating ice are breached by isolated nunataks, the peaks of mighty mountains that are just clearing the surface.* (1975)

BELOW *A typical situation where one-year-old sea-ice has failed to break away from the shelf-ice in the distance. The ice will be one to two metres thick and impassable for any but the heaviest icebreaker.* (1947)

LEFT *This view looking northwards over Neny Fjord was taken in 1966 as part of an aerial survey of the Antarctic Peninsula. The Debenham Islands and Stonington Island are in the middle distance, to the east of the most prominent island in the photograph. The high peaks of Adelaide Island showing above the cloud are about 70 miles away.*

Much of the Wordie Ice Shelf is a maze of great rifts created by the rapidly-deforming ice. The ones shown here are probably about 20 metres wide and 30 metres deep and would swallow half-a-dozen double-decker buses without any problem. (1973)

Going South

THE SEAS THAT SURROUND ANTARCTICA are dangerous and unpredictable. The inhospitable conditions on the continent itself – snow, extreme cold, biting winds, periods of continuous darkness – are here augmented by the additional hazards of ocean currents, moving masses of floating ice and fog. The slow-moving glaciers that originate on the polar plateau push out across the sea as floating shelf-ice, often a mile thick and hundreds of miles wide. The shelf-ice breaks off into enormous flat tabular icebergs, which drift slowly in the ocean currents, uncharted and unchartable. Lesser glaciers calve off into smaller bergs, 'bergy bits', which combine with the freezing winter sea to form pack-ice, sometimes thick and impenetrable, sometimes open and navigable, but never the same two days together.

The shores of the Antarctic Peninsula were first sighted nearly a century ago by the skilful and courageous captains of sealing and whaling ships who worked southwards through the offshore islands to anchorages on the west side of the Peninsula itself. In the Weddell Sea on the east of the Peninsula the ocean current circulates clockwise, gathering and concentrating the pack-ice from the far south and sweeping it slowly and relentlessly northwards along the coast of the Peninsula. These are very dangerous waters and of the three ships that penetrated the Weddell Sea before 1948 and sighted the coast only one returned. Ships can approach the west side of the Peninsula more easily as here there is open water for much of the year. The general trend of the current on the west is southwards, gathering the loose pack released from the Weddell Sea, combining it with ice from the shorter, west-flowing glaciers and forming areas of dangerous, unstable, treacherous pack. The

PREVIOUS PAGE *RRS* Bransfield, *the palatial flagship of the British Antarctic Survey. Her rounded hull means she performs well in ice but she is a pig in the open sea. Here, off Rothera base, the water is too deep for her to anchor so she is unloading while under way, keeping a channel open for the scows that are taking the cargo ashore.* (1976)

pattern of ice movement round the northern tip of the Peninsula is different every year – sometimes the ice edge moves northwards to surround the islands of South Georgia, the South Shetlands and the South Orkneys with dense pack; sometimes it fails to move, leaving areas of open, ice-free sea. Conditions vary considerably from year to year and from day to day. Sometimes the sea never freezes and ships can penetrate far inside the Antarctic Circle, sometimes the ice never moves away from the coast and a ship's captain can see his destination but never reach it. Gale-force winds from the high mountains can change the picture overnight, consolidating or breaking up ice and making access to the coast difficult and anchorages dangerous. It is incredible to think that these were the waters penetrated by sailing ships a century ago in their search for whales and it is humbling for today's travellers to anchor beneath a painted sign recording the visit of a sailing brig one hundred years earlier.

Ships are the key to all the work that goes on in the Antarctic. Though it can be justifiably claimed that aircraft have opened up the continent, without ships to bring in the fuel that they need the Antarctic would be relatively unexplored. Ships also provide vital support for all scientific work, bringing in men and equipment and relieving bases during the summer months.

This chapter is about reaching the continent, the ships that sailed south and the problems that were faced in getting there – in landing stores, vehicles and men. In the fifty years covered by this book there have been enormous changes in the size and power of the ships that go south, as the diagram shows only too clearly. But there has also been considerable progress in other areas – ship's masters have become more skilful in handling their ships and keeping clear of trouble, charts have improved, and automatic depth recorders that can look forwards as well as downwards have replaced the hand-held leadlines that were still in use in 1947. As recently as the 1950s a ship's captain relied on the crow's nest to provide limited sight over the horizon and much of the skill of the good 'ice-captain' lay in his instinctive understanding of 'iceblink', whether the undersides of distant clouds showed black, indicating open water, or if they appeared white, in which case dense pack lay ahead. Radar now gives him long-range eyes and helps him to pilot safely through narrow, fog-bound channels. Satellite photographs are also used as an aid to navigation. They are consulted daily in the United Kingdom and the ship's master is told where to steer to find open water.

Although navigation is now easier the problems involved in day-to-day ship handling are as demanding as ever. The captain still has to decide whether to use the ship's power to bash on through hard pack-ice or to save fuel by waiting patiently for the wind and weather to break the ice up for him. He will still have to decide how to place his ship in worsening weather so that stores can be unloaded quickly. In the period covered by this book no ship came to grief, no lives have been lost at sea, and only once, in 1949, has a base been left unsupplied with stores. This is a measure of the debt that all those who have worked in the Antarctic owe to the captains of the ships who sail south.

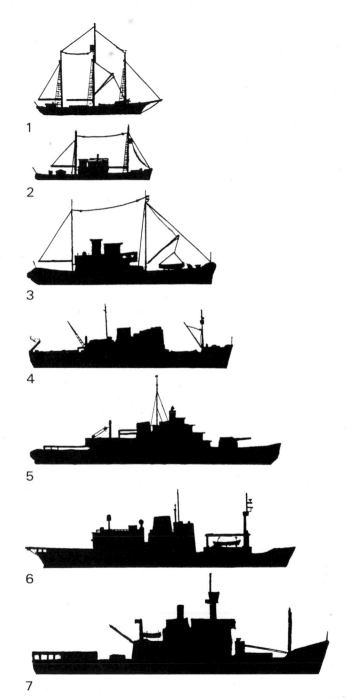

RIGHT *How ships have changed.*
1 Penola *(1934–7). 31 m, 210 tonnes, 60 HP.*
2 MV Trepassey *(1945–7). 37.5 m, 320 tonnes, 400 HP.*
3 *RRS* John Biscoe I *(1947–55) and MV* Port of Beaumont *(1946–8). 56 m, 899 tonnes, 750 HP.*
4 *RRS* John Biscoe II *(1956–82). 66 m, 1584 tonnes, 1350 HP.*
5 *USS* Edisto *and USS* Burton Island *(1948). 82 m, 5500 tonnes, 22000 HP.*
6 *HMS* Endurance *(1968–82). 93m, 3220 tonnes, 1600 HP.*
7 *RRS* Bransfield *(1970–82). 99 m, 4816 tonnes, 3200 HP.*

Accessibility by sea is one of the factors that affects the siting of a base. Here Adelaide base has been iced in by an onshore wind and RRS Bransfield *is lying out to sea waiting for conditions to change. Four days later an offshore wind gave open water close to the shore.* (1974)

The pack-ice near RRS Bransfield could be described as 'medium' – and her reinforced bows are making good progress through it. In the middle distance the ice looks much thicker and it will be much harder work. As long as there is some open water, a well-found ship can push her way through open pack. When the sea is completely frozen over progress is very slow as the bows have to ride over the ice, letting the propeller wash take the broken pieces underneath the ship and out of the way. (1976)

LEFT *The* Penola, *a wooden three-masted topsail schooner bought by the British Graham Land Expedition for £3000. Although only five of her thirteen-man crew had any previous sea-going experience, she made the 7500 miles to the Falkland Islands in 74 days. Most of the passage was under sail with the auxiliary engines being reserved for windless days or working in and out of harbour. This picture was taken in the Doldrums on her way south. (1934)*

Penola *was allowed to freeze in for the first winter in a sheltered cove well protected from the pressures of moving sea-ice. In the spring the members of the expedition worked day-and-night shifts for three days sawing the ice up and pushing the pieces out of the creek to free the ship. (1935)*

LEFT *In 1946, the Ronne Antarctic Research Expedition sailed south in the wooden* Port of Beaumont *which was manned by an amateur crew. At that time no aircraft could fly directly to Antarctica and so they were carried as deck cargo, together with their fuel.*

BELOW LEFT *Navigating by radar through scattered ice, driving sleet and thick fog in the half-mile-wide Lemaire Channel. The precipitous sides of the channel were never visible but fortunately this is a well-charted and deep passage. (1974)*

Watching the bows of a ship working through ice is always interesting and from the crow's nest the skill of the helmsman can be appreciated. Here the bows are about to hit the larger ice-floe and they will be thrown sharply to the right into the open space to starboard. The wedge action of the bows will push the floes apart and the old course will be resumed. (1975)

LEFT *At one stage in the 1934–7 expedition the* Penola *was used to establish a second base 200 miles further south. The route was inside the shelter of the floating ice and the deck cargo was not as well stored as would be necessary for a proper sea passage. The expedition motor launch in the foreground is full of empty crates, while petrol drums for the aircraft fill every spare corner. (1936)*

ABOVE RIGHT *In 1945 the Falkland Islands Dependencies Survey charted MV Trepassey for the season. She was a brand new ship built to trade on the Labrador coast and it was a very long haul to Antarctica. She was not much larger than the* Penola, *beamier, and with a good deal more cargo space. In 1946 she landed three years' stores for ten men and the next year brought down an aircraft as deck cargo. (1946)*

BELOW RIGHT *In 1947 the Falkland Islands Dependencies Survey commissioned the wooden* John Biscoe I *and she did sterling service for five years, even though her fine bows tended to cut through the ice rather than ride over it. On her return to Port Stanley at the end of the 1948 season the ship's side was less than 25 millimetres thick in places!*

At the newly-built Rothera base in 1976 a lot of work had to be done to find the best route for getting the cargo ashore. Floating ice and underwater rocks combine to make all inshore work fraught with problems but, while rocks can be charted, moving pieces of ice, often weighing tens of tonnes, frequently halted the process of landing supplies. Launches, scows and stores had to be guarded jealously – replacements were 8500 miles away. (1976)

LEFT *A ship cannot be steered if it is moving slowly without engines.* Burton Island *passed lines aboard* Port of Beaumont *and drew her bow tight against the matting fender on the* Burton Island's *stern. This gave the icebreaker complete control over the* Beaumont *while it was being towed. (1947)*

LEFT *In the 1947–8 season the sea-ice was slow to break up and it is doubtful if the shore party would have been relieved without the help of the US navy. Here the two monster US icebreakers are breaking up the ice before taking* Port of Beaumont *in tow. In the distance is the edge of the 'fast' ice ten miles away. (1947)*

RIGHT *Here the US icebreaker* Burton Island *is backing down to the bows of* Port of Beaumont *to take her in tow. (1947)*

In the South Orkneys in 1972 the ice was strong
enough close inshore to allow the relief ship to unload
on to sledges within 180 metres of the base. This
relief, measured in hours rather than days or even
weeks, was one of the quickest ever recorded.

This is how stores are usually unloaded, using open scows. It is very hard work towing the scow through this sort of sea-ice – it looks well broken up but the water in between the floes will probably be refreezing and the consistency of porridge. (1974)

ABOVE *For really rapid handling of cargo there is very little to beat a 'human chain'. Here the scow is at the ice edge and coal sacks are being unloaded at the rate of about a tonne every four to five minutes, but it requires very accurate timing to get the chain working with a precise rhythm. The standard cry as the last sack leaves the scow is always the same: 'That is the one we are looking for!' (1978)*

By law, flammable cargo has to be carried on deck. These drums on the Bransfield *are the petrol stocks to last six BAS bases for one year and they hide several thousand other drums of the less dangerous aircraft fuel which is stored in the hold. A damaged and leaking drum could lead to a major disaster and drums as deck cargo have to be packed tightly to prevent movement in heavy weather. (1974)*

*How bulk fuel was landed at Rothera. This ship got so
close to the shore that by pumping all the ballast
forward she was able to get her bows firmly on a
shelf of rock and hoses were connected to the large
fuel tanks ashore. (1976)*

Home from Home

IT IS 7.30 AM at a six-man Antarctic base at 72° south. It is five weeks after midwinter's day – it is dark outside and has been 24 hours a day for the last ten weeks. It is only morning because the ringing alarm clock says so. A man climbs out of his bunk and walks over to the cooking stove, pausing as he passes to examine the cluster of weather-recording instruments mounted on the hut wall. The 60-mile-an-hour wind of the last few days has gone, the temperature outside has dropped 30°C in the last 14 hours to − 40°C and the barometer is rising fast. High winds play havoc with even the best thermostats and the stove is very hot – at least the kettle will boil quickly.

He gets breakfast by battery lights and at 8 am puts five cups of tea on the table and gives his own version of 'Wakey! Wakey!' With luck six men will be sitting down to breakfast by 8.15 am – porridge, cooked overnight in the bottom oven, bacon and hot bread rolls. Half-way through breakfast the duty met man will disappear as he is already twenty minutes adrift with his morning readings.

It is Saturday, 'barrack room sports' day when all work ceases until the whole base has been cleaned. This is a tradition that goes back to the days when all expeditions were run by the Navy and ensures that standards are maintained. By mid-morning 'sports' are finished and the day's jobs are discussed over elevenses. The diesel is due for servicing, there is a seal carcase to be collected that is needed for dog food and there is obvious trouble with the wind generator which has got out of balance and was shaking itself to pieces in the gale. Jobs seem to get allocated – no one person is giving orders. A base that appears to run itself in this way is a well-run and probably happy base.

PREVIOUS PAGE *The return of the sun at Fossil Bluff. The winter darkness starts to lighten in late July and although the sun is still below the horizon here, mother-of-pearl clouds like these indicate that it will soon be visible. These clouds are estimated to be some 19 to 25 miles above the earth's surface and are rarely seen elsewhere in the world. (1975)*

The hut empties leaving the cook making bread and the day's wireless operator sending off the weather. Reception is so good that he is chatting up the base 125 miles further north where they have just seen the sun for the first time after the long winter. Although the sun is not due here for a further four or five days, a shout from outside tells him to look out. Far to the north and very high in the sky a cloud is lit from underneath by a sun that is still well below the horizon. It is absolutely calm and ice forms in his nostrils as he breathes.

After the gales of the last few days, there is a lot to be done. The huskies need feeding and the water-supply tank next to the stove needs filling. Blocks of wind-packed snow will do but these don't make much water and the man whose turn it is for a bath that night is going to hitch up a dog team to collect a box or two of ice chippings from a local iceberg. Lunch is a simple meal – soup, fresh bread rolls, jam and cheese. The wireless operator relays the latest gossip from other bases and gives someone a personal message from home received via the main base's telex. Work continues in the afternoon and the promise of hot crumpets for tea brings everyone in on time.

By evening everyone is round the table. Someone is repairing windproofs with a sewing machine, a surveyor is ruling up some field sheets, two dog-drivers are arguing about a proposed modification to a dog harness, and someone else is trying to repair the windcharger propeller with a mixture of sawdust and araldite. Supper is a relaxed and civilized meal, with a tablecloth. Cooking is by rota and the week's cook is spurred on by the knowledge that he will be at the eating end five weeks out of six. After supper life becomes more social and there is often a game of scrabble or chess. There may be a bit of background music or the BBC world service may be turned on. At 10 pm the diesel will be stopped and everyone retires to his bunk. Some may read for a while by their personal battery lights but by midnight all will be asleep.

This description of a day at base could be anywhere, but there is no such thing as a typical base as each is very individual. Since the 1930s the most obvious change has been in the degree of comfort and in the sophistication of the equipment provided. Early expedition budgets were very tight, ships were small and base huts were no larger than absolutely necessary. By the 1960s money was less restricted, ships were larger and expeditions were less short-term. As time went by it became possible to undertake long-term scientific projects and bases were and still are staffed on a more permanent basis involving annual reliefs in order to take off occupants and replenish stores. Each year huts have been better made, better insulated, better equipped, more comfortable and more expensive.

The process of setting up a base is far more complex than simply building a hut and ensuring that it is materially well found and adequately supplied. The ideal site will be accessible by sea for annual re-supply and there will be a suitable airstrip nearby that will not be plagued by weather problems. It will also be a good centre for the proposed scientific fieldwork with easy access to the mainland (most bases are sited on islands offshore). Chosen sites are always a compromise and the final decision will be made in consultation with the ship's master, on whom so many other responsibilities rest.

The six bases pictured here are a good cross-section. In 1936 the British Graham Land Expedition's southern base was used for one winter only and was abandoned in 1937. The Stonington Island base of the Falkland Islands Dependencies Survey was built in 1946 and occupied on and off until it was finally closed in 1975. Fossil Bluff, built in 1961, is a four-man advance base to provide a centre for glaciological research and has an excellent airstrip and relatively stable weather conditions. Adelaide base was originally built in 1961 when ice made the planned site inaccessible. After being enlarged several times, it was closed in 1977 partly because it had outlived its usefulness but mostly because of the break up of the airstrip. It was replaced by the complex built at Rothera Point, also on Adelaide Island. The present Bird Island base hut was only built in 1982. It is a centre for wildlife studies on the northern edge of the Antarctic and, in the sense that one cannot get away, it is the most isolated of all.

This chapter shows how the values that applied in the period 1934–7 have evolved into the way bases are run today. British Antarctic bases have a well-earned reputation for being well-organized, well-run and effective, and also for being happy. Whatever the material conditions, a successful base is very largely a question of selecting the right people and setting the right standards. When these are right they are truly a home from home.

ABOVE *The British Graham Land Expedition built its southern base on the Debenham Islands. The leader had spotted them from the air and thought they looked as if they would provide a good anchorage for Penola, while a raised beach on the largest island looked like being a splendid site for a base hut. The sea was expected to freeze solid for much of the year providing easy access for field journeys further south. As it turned out the sea-ice proved unpredictable and limited the expedition's field travels considerably. (1936)*

RIGHT *The southern base was built from old timbers recovered from the derelict whaling station on Deception Island and the shore party lived in tents while it was being constructed. Note the dogs tethered to anything strong enough to hold them. (1936)*

LEFT *In the spring of 1936 the sea was well frozen but the southern base was not unduly drifted up in spite of the 100-knot winds that came at frequent intervals from the glacier off to the left. The hangar at the near end of the hut could take the aircraft with its wings folded. The aircraft would be mounted on skis once the ground was snow-covered and the airstrip was the smooth sea-ice between the base and the glacier.*

ABOVE *The BGLE's southern base was still snow-free when it was visited in 1946 – a tribute to the leader's choice of position as a badly-sited hut would have drifted over in this time.*

In 1945 the Falkland Islands
Dependencies Survey built the
Stonington base six miles south of
the Debenhams. In 1947 when the
photograph above was taken the
sea froze early and remained solid
so far into the season that it was
touch and go whether the base
would be relieved. The icebergs in
the distance were the base's water
supply – two boxes of ice chippings
each day met all needs. The dogs
were always tethered out, whatever
the weather.

ABOVE RIGHT 28 years later at the
same time of year the sea is open.
Changing ice conditions from year
to year made it very difficult to plan
fieldwork and by 1970 an inland
route south had been found which
eliminated the need to use
treacherous sea-ice for routine
travel. (1974)

When the sea is frozen, Stonington Island hardly seems to be an island at all. The FIDS huts are close to the shoreline on the left with some American huts between them and the ramp up to the glacier (the only route off the island until the sea froze). (1946)

ABOVE LEFT *A great deal of time at base was spent on dog training in the early years. The dog expert of the 1934 expedition, 'Doc' Bingham, was leader for the first year at Stonington Island and set very high standards. Here a dog and a bitch are breathless after a fast training run. (1946)*

ABOVE RIGHT *At base the dogs were fed 2 to 3 kilogrammes of seal every other day. This meant killing and bringing back to base about 300 seals a year. Nobody enjoyed this job but all base members soon became experts and could kill and clean a seal in about two minutes. (1945)*

LEFT *During the three weeks that* Trepassey *was unloading stores Stonington Island base was built and occupied. The foundations took three or four days but once the floor had been laid the frame went up very quickly. Working eighteen hours a day, by the tenth day the main hut was weather-proof and the base was complete in twenty-four days. (1946)*

Huskies love pulling – the trick is to train them to pull in the right direction. If the lead dog can be taught to turn by word of mouth the rest will follow and on this training run in 1945 the driver, Kevin Walton, had a long whip that could reach the lead dog 15 metres ahead. With luck, after a year or so, this team would turn on a coin, pull like a tractor or stop dead in their tracks following a spoken command. Only then would they be fit for work in the field. Today it is no longer economical to have dog teams but it is a matter of policy to have dogs around as they are good for morale. (1945)

In summer, the base hut at Stonington Island was no longer covered in snow. By 1946 a second-hand Nissen hut had been added for stores and it also included the luxury of a bathroom and a 'loo'. The base was registered as a post office and boasted the only double-glazed greenhouse in Antarctica. (1946)

In the 1930s and 40s the size of base hut largely depended on the size of the expedition ship. Huts were pretty basic, consisting of a large central room with open bunks on three sides. In the evening scene at the 1947 base (ABOVE CENTRE) the wireless operator is writing up his log, the surveyor is sewing up some cold-weather silk gloves and the base leader is sorting out some stores' lists with help from two onlookers. ABOVE *In a small base it is impossible to carry a full-time cook but expedition members, in this case Launcelot Fleming, became remarkably proficient. Aga-type stoves like this one are still used for cooking. (1936)*

ABOVE RIGHT *The doctor in his bunk. (1936)*

FAR RIGHT *A daily chore was to take the rubbish to the tide crack where the movement of the sea-ice grinds it up into small pieces. (1947)*

RIGHT *The 'loo' with a view – the wires held it down in 100-knot gales and it was sufficiently draughty to discourage malingerers. (1947)*

In a single-roomed hut the only privacy is to be found in one's bunk and this takes on the character of its inhabitant. It is understood that anyone who has retired to his bunk has withdrawn from whatever else is going on. (1974)

Although Fossil Bluff is so small, it is an excellent example of efficient space utilization. Most home-comforts are available, including a record-deck, books, magazines (usually at least two years out of date), and electric light. (1974)

Adelaide base was originally built in 1961 but was steadily enlarged over the years and became a main base, housing thirteen men through the winter and up to thirty-five during the summer season. In a base as large as this there are specialists – radio operators, *meteorologists, mechanics and a cook. This is Christmas 1974 and a mammoth nine-course meal is about to begin with everyone in shirts and ties. In 1977 the base was closed and was replaced by a new base at Rothera some 38 miles away.*

Sledges arrive at base as a kit of wooden parts and need to be assembled before they can be used. The parts are literally lashed together using either dope-tightened string or rawhide thongs. The lashings and the carefully-selected ash of which the sledge is made allow the structure to flex as it travels heavy-laden over rough surfaces. (1974)

Fossil Bluff is not large enough to have specialists and here everyone is expected to take a turn at everything. For nine months of the year the radio was the only link with the outside world – all telexes went from the UK to Adelaide base and were then passed on verbally. Here Jim Bishop has just made contact with the main base. (1974)

ABOVE *The winter snows cover up much of the almost inevitable mess round any Antarctic base and turn it into a scenic spot. Here at Fossil Bluff the main hut is on the right and the two huts at the other end of the 'High Street' serve as store and garage. The tent in the middle is the 'loo' – a very cold spot in winter. The prominent peak is 'Pyramid', 800 metres high and a favourite destination for an afternoon stroll.* (1975)

RIGHT *Fossil Bluff is a small base, a single-roomed hut 6 metres by 4 metres that is home to four men. This typical winter scene was taken by flash and shows half-buried food boxes, drums of diesel for the small generator, and the sledges on the roof.* (1974)

*A year's stores outside Fossil Bluff.
This photographic record will
show where to dig for what in
midwinter when the base is snow-
covered. Note the sledges on the
hut roof and the heavy steel cables
to hold the hut down in high wind.
(1975)*

Camping equipment and food for field parties is checked with great care. The pots' and pans' box (RIGHT) contains everything necessary to live comfortably at low temperatures in a tent, including a tin of spare parts for the Primus stove and Tilley lamp. Fuel for light and heat is paraffin, with meths to help get things going. A day's rations (BELOW RIGHT) weigh about 900 grammes but contain as much as 4200 calories. They include porridge oats, chocolate, soup powder, dried meat, dried onion, potato powder, biscuits and butter, tea bags, cocoa and milk powder. (1975)

This garage, built in the Falklands, was dismantled and flown into Fossil Bluff and was a late but vital addition to the base. With three Muskeg tractors, six skidoos and numerous portable generators to maintain the mechanic was kept busy all winter – bitterly cold work in a garage without insulation. (1974)

In 1976 a start was made on the new base on Adelaide Island, at Rothera Point. This was intended to house a wintering party of ten to twelve and up to forty people in the summer. By 1979 it had grown to four substantial buildings which had excellent facilities of all kinds – mechanical, scientific, medical, culinary – and comfortable space for relaxation.

The new base hut built on Bird Island in 1982 had to be put in the middle of a 20,000-strong seal colony. Unloading was only possible after a barrier of petrol drums had been erected against curious seals.

Because of improved living conditions at base, less time has to be spent in running a base efficiently. A four-man base still means that everyone takes turns with the cooking, but in the 1982 Bird Island kitchen seen here the job is far simpler than it was in the 1936 kitchen pictured earlier. Both use Aga-type stoves for cooking.

Travelling Overland

THE TWO-MAN PARTY with their seventeen dogs and two sledges were relieved to reach the safety of the Refuge Islands. They were at the end of a very successful field trip and base was now only about 12 miles away. When they had set off twelve hours earlier it had been a cloudless day and they had taken a calculated risk in deciding to drive over the sea-ice straight for the offshore islands rather than taking the longer and possibly safer route closer inshore. By early afternoon they had made very good progress and had 22 miles of the 25-mile stretch behind them with only one minor diversion to avoid a seal lying out on the ice – the dogs would have gone berserk if they had seen it and the party was not in need of extra dog food.

Then things had started to go wrong. The lead dog broke through the ice which was less solid than it looked, the offshore wind was now noticeable and was obviously going to increase, loose surface snow was beginning to lift and the dogs were reluctant to hold their course without having a man walking in front. This had meant leaving the dogs to pull the second sledge on their own with no one to steer it through the belt of pressure ice. Then the ice had started to break up and long cracks appeared that made the dogs hesitate. It had all become very tense with the sledges having to be used as bridges where the leads were too wide to be jumped over. It had turned really cold, with a temperature of about $-30°C$ and with a strong wind blowing off the land. But now the party had reached the islands and they were able to relax.

The next morning the sea-ice had gone and they were marooned and unable to move. They were also very lucky. Fortunately for them the Refuge Islands had lived up to

PREVIOUS PAGE *Camp has been pitched. The tractor train and skidoo stand out in the elements while Fossil Bluff's retired husky, Rasmus, is looking for the most comfortable spot to shelter from the rising wind. Each pyramid tent houses two men in a cosy 2-metre-square den. The wind will be whining round the guy-ropes but the insulated tents will be warm and snug. (1974)*

their name and there was also an emergency cache of food. If the sea-ice had remained fast they would have been back to base in less than half a day – now they might just as well be 100 miles away and they could well have to stay put until the annual relief ship arrived!

The 800-mile journey that was behind them had involved typically varied travelling conditions. Their route had lain inland from the base, travelling first over sea-ice and then up on to the central plateau of the Peninsula by way of one of the many glaciers that fall to the sea over its edge. On the outward journey, surfaces had been initially smooth, hard and very fast and although the glacier was heavily crevassed severe winds had left good snow bridges over the majority of them. Sadly, however, two dogs had fallen into a crevasse and only one had been recovered alive.

Once on the plateau, conditions changed. They had been held up by day after day of cloud and whiteout, both of which tend to persist here because of the conflicting weather patterns on either side of the Peninsula. When travel was possible the hoar-frost surface that had looked so perfect had proved to be more like desert sand. But on the way back their luck had changed once again. Broadly speaking, the higher the terrain the more predictable the travelling as the snow surface never melts at high altitudes and on the way home day after day of cloudless weather had given the party runs of over 25 miles a day on the plateau.

All journeys in the Antarctic involve a range of surfaces and weather conditions and the aim of all travel is to use the right equipment in the right way at the right time. The earliest photographs date from the time when huskies were the main means of transport in the field. Some members of the British Graham Land Expedition had a background of working with huskies in Greenland and they were anxious to extend their expertise to the Antarctic. At that time, too, mechanical vehicles were little better than mildly-modified farm tractors.

Although dogs are no longer used, they are still the only form of transport that can cope safely with all the conditions that arise in the Antarctic. Dogs can swim and jump and if they fall into a crevasse they can usually be pulled out. On the other hand, they do need to be well trained and they are slow. Moreover, they need to be fed whether they are travelling or not. The last dog teams worked in the field in 1975 and since then only mechanical transport has been used.

Now the range of vehicles that is available is so wide that something can be found to cover most of the conditions that can be expected in the field apart from sea-ice. Sea-ice travel is never safe and has been responsible for most of the accidental deaths in the Antarctic, but the chances of survival are enormously increased in a party with well-trained dogs.

In general, sea-ice travel is avoided today. This has only been possible with air support, as aircraft are now used to ferry parties and their equipment from base into the field so that it is no longer necessary to travel over sea-ice. For this reason, it is vital that modern bases are sited with easy access to a suitable airstrip.

Although the means of transport have changed enormously in the last fifty years, there are still many parallels between travelling in the 1930s and the 1980s. The cold is no less cold, the price paid for mistakes no less high and parties can still be held up for weeks waiting for the weather to clear. And the satisfaction gained from completing a field journey is as great as ever.

In 1946 the expedition based at Stonington Island was faced with the task of crossing the 2000-metre plateau to survey the east coast of the Peninsula. The route to the plateau was up a glacier at a slope of 1 in 2½ and this is what it looked like from the top. The camp is about half a mile away.

LEFT *Here a well-trained dog team is working through pressure ice. The driver is having problems keeping the sledge upright but the dogs are enjoying it immensely. (1946)*

ABOVE *Here four teams of nine dogs are making good progress in splendid snow conditions on a plateau crossing (see previous caption). If the loads were heavy it often paid to couple two teams together and take things at a trot. For safety on downhill runs thick rope was wound round the runners so that the teams had to pull the sledges down. In moderate conditions the plateau crossing would take three days but it has taken thirty in dense cloud or gale-force winds. (1974)*

There will always be situations where man-hauling is the most effective form of motive power. Here in South Georgia the distances are not great and two months' stores are being hauled over the Ross Pass. The surface was hard blue ice and the wind over 60 mph. The men are wearing crampons – but they still fell over. (1950)

In whiteout conditions poorly-trained dog teams lose heart. Whiteout is not the same as fog: a dark object can be seen many metres away but there are no shadows and here the leading team could well be about to walk over a high cliff or run into a snow drift. In the event this team was steered by compass with such accuracy that after 15 miles they were only 150 metres off course. The lead dog on this occasion was Darkie who had been trained by 'Doc' Bingham, the 1946 base leader. Darkie was almost human in his instinct for avoiding danger and any new driver was on probation until Darkie had satisfied himself that he was competent. (1946)

ABOVE *Glacier travel demands constant vigilance and the need always to be roped up to something, as crevasses are often snow-covered and invisible. Here in South Georgia a sledge is being used as a four-metre bridge to cross a crevasse. (1951)*

RIGHT *Antarctic travel is a snail's existence – everything needs to be carried 'on one's back'. This sledge is loaded with food for 20 days, petrol for 150 skidoo miles, full camping gear, emergency and rescue equipment, radio and scientific instruments. Nothing must be left out as apparently trivial omissions can have serious consequences. This is a typically beautiful winter midday sky – temperature about –30°C. (1974)*

RIGHT *Late on in the summer the snow lying on sea-ice starts to melt and forms pools of fresh water on the surface. While many will refreeze, some will melt right through or remain as shallow pools. Here some puddles were frozen sufficiently to carry a dog's weight, but not the loaded sledges or the drivers, who are getting very wet. It is possible to drive a sledge across the leads between ice-floes provided the channel is not more than half the length of the sledge. (1936)*

BELOW *Offshore winds and currents can play havoc with a sea-ice surface and transform good conditions into a nightmare in a matter of hours. This nine-dog team is pulling a light load on hard windblown snow lying on sea-ice – a traveller's paradise. Only a week later the pilot of a light aircraft landed on the same bit of sea-ice and fell through. (1946)*

ABOVE *Ten men, six sledges and forty-three dogs are on a long haul to the plateau from the Larsen Ice Shelf 1700 metres below. This area was known to be crevasse-free and it was necessary to move fast to take advantage of the weather. The 30-mile plateau crossing was completed in 7½ hours – months before it had taken 30 days. (1946)*

RIGHT *When in crevassed country with several vehicles and sledges it is wise to keep them roped together for safety. In this enormous train three skidoos are towing four sledges in tandem over the featureless Bach Ice Shelf, some 125 miles from Fossil Bluff. (1974)*

LEFT *In 1936 two 500-mile journeys were made with dogs. At this night-camp they are tethered to the sledge while they finish off their pemmican ration. The dogs are of mixed Labrador and Greenland stock. Many were born in Antarctica and some were pups of the team leader on the right.*

LEFT *The start of a 500-mile two-month journey. The Muskeg tractor was driven 62 miles south of Fossil Bluff and was then abandoned while the three skidoos crossed Alexander Island. The guard's van at the rear of the tractor train is a caboose – a sort of tent-substitute. The fuel drums are for the tractor – with this load it averages about 1 mpg! (1974)*

ABOVE *The 'blow' has only been going a few hours but already drifts have started to form round the skidoo. Here the engine is being covered over to prevent the snow clogging it up. (1973)*

A skidoo is much more efficient than a dog team but it is noisy and very thirsty for fuel. Here the second man of a two-man party is riding a loaded sledge which carries all the camping equipment (ABOVE LEFT). At the end of a morning the party will stop and erect the small pup tent carried by the skidoo to give warmth and shelter for a lunch halt (LEFT). (1974)

Here the Muskeg is pulling a very heavy train of four sledges. It was a warm day and sitting on top of the caboose, camera in hand, was a very comfortable place to be. The train was moving at about 3 mph so the driver could leave the Muskeg occasionally and come back for a chat. (1974)

In 1934 a small air-cooled Bristol tractor was given to the expedition and was used round base with great success until it broke through the sea-ice. It was brought to the surface after four months and ran better than before but subsequently had to be abandoned on a journey when the sea-ice broke up. On good surfaces it had a pull equivalent to six teams of dogs.

During World War II amphibious tracked vehicles were developed for jungle warfare and when modified for cold climates these proved to work splendidly in snow. They should have been good on sea-ice, but although they floated they could not crawl out if they broke through. (1946)

*These two sledge parties (*RIGHT *1936,* BELOW *1974) are separated by over forty years and show how little this aspect of Antarctic life has changed. The sledges look the same, ration boxes are still standard and the tent on top is still there. In good weather the routine is still to use the sledge as a shelter while drinking hot soup from a thermos. Even the clothing is similar – large, baggy and wind-proof with wolverine fur round the head.*

Life in the Field

GIVE A MAN A RIFLE, some ammunition, some furs, a snow-knife, and lots of experience and he will survive in the Arctic. This is not true of the Antarctic Continent, which is devoid of wildlife of any kind. The surrounding oceans may be teeming with wildlife but they only come ashore briefly to breed. The Antarctic traveller must carry everything he needs, or might need, with him and must know how to use every piece of equipment if he is to survive. Living in the field demands enormous attention to detail, adherence to rules and routines and the ability of the party to be self-sufficient and self-reliant, able to get themselves out of trouble when it arrives, as it surely will.

Imagine a field party of four men with two sledges and skidoos at the end of a long day's travel. They are trying to make distance quickly after thirty days in the field and have come some 40 miles, helped by a following wind. It is autumn and the nights are already longer than the days. To make camp the two sledges are drawn up alongside with 20 metres between them and facing down-wind. Now they have stopped, the men find the wind far stronger than they had realized and as a precaution all four take a hand in unloading and putting up each tent. The wind makes talking impossible but it doesn't matter because they are well-practised. Ration boxes or snow blocks will be used to weigh down the skirts and the few pegs will be well trodden into the snow. The two 'inside men' for the day are impatient to get into the tents – it is cold and the longer they remain outside the longer the other two must wait. Once inside each man will sweep all traces of snow off his clothes and then shout for the sleeping bags and cooking box to be passed in. With windproofs off and

socks changed he will slide into his sleeping bag and start the evening brew. The men outside have been discussing unloading the sledges to prevent them drifting over but they have decided to take the risk of leaving them as they are. Anything that would be easily detached and lost – skis, tripod, crevasse probe and snow shoes – are stacked upright and tied together. The boxes of scientific instruments are double checked to see that they are sealed properly against drifting snow.

Snow blocks have been cut and placed by the entrance sleeves, the can of paraffin sits between the tents and well clear of the snow to be used for water, a wireless aerial has been set up. After a last look round to see all is secure, the outside man will park his shovel by the entrance to his tent and push his way in. Inside all is warm. He will brush off any loose snow before it melts, slide out of his windproofs and change his socks before he too gets into his sleeping bag. With practice this whole exercise may take only 15 minutes.

With luck there will be a mug of tea waiting for him and there is an appetising smell of the evening meal. High protein food with a high fat content is made more palatable by the addition of onion flakes or bacon pieces; sometimes the brew is sloppy like soup, sometimes thick like porridge. There is a slight crackle from the wireless which has been left on to pick up the BBC world service or a call from base. The day's survey notes will need to be written up or some ice-movement calculations completed. The soothing noise of the Primus will cease when cooking is finished and the pressure lamp will take over the job of keeping the tent warm and drying the socks and gloves hanging in the peak. Sleeping bags are really warm with inflatable air mattresses and sheepskin as extra protection against the cold: the four men will soon be snoring peacefully.

The sound of the morning alarm sets the whole process into reverse. Getting up too sharply means a morning bath of hoar-frost so the cook will use one hand to light the Primus and both men will watch the frost-line creep down the side of the tent as the air warms up. Breakfast is porridge, half-prepared the night before. Dead on time the two outside men push their way through their tent

PREVIOUS PAGE *A hard-packed snow surface means that, although the wind is blowing strongly, very little snow is drifting. If it weren't for the fact that it's −20°C and the gale is 25 knots this would be a good day for fieldwork. The call sign for this party is sledge 'W-Whisky' – the home-made flag depicts the letter W and an upturned bottle! (1975)*

sleeves – where the sledges had been there are now white mounds of drifted snow. There is a lot of digging to be done and it is two, maybe three hours after the alarm has gone off before they are on the move. They will travel for three hours, have a long break for lunch, and then move on for another four hours. If it is a good day they will make perhaps 40 miles but if wind and weather have turned against them it could be only half that distance with ten times the effort.

There is a certain timelessness about work in the field and, apart from the means of transport being skidoos not huskies, this account could apply equally well to the 1930s or the 1980s. The things that have changed are the distances travelled, the nature of the work done, the reliance on aircraft for support and, of course, the introduction of reliable, two-way wireless communication. Early fieldwork was truly exploratory in that the primary task was to map and survey the surface outlines of the continent. Today surveying is more likely to be concerned with measuring ice deformation and movement than topographical features, while other scientific projects may include extracting ice samples from depth or mapping the sub-ice landscape. Field parties may be held up for days waiting for conditions in which readings can be taken but the long delays involved in scientific work are offset by the increased speed of travel.

This chapter is about what it is like to live in the field and the sort of work that is done. In contrast to life at base, fieldwork is the one way to get really close to the Antarctic in all its moods and contrasts and to appreciate fully the majesty of the continent.

LEFT *In November 1975 four glaciologists left Fossil Bluff to cross the Peninsula with the aim of obtaining information about the snow on the plateau. This is the first camp of the trip, next to an impressive 300-metre rock tower, and the team are enjoying an afternoon break soaking up the sun in front of the tents.*

ABOVE *On a glacier swept by gale-strength winds the actual siting of a camp is very important. As the scoop below the ridge in the photograph is entirely wind-blown, it would probably have paid to site camp nearer the rock face on the left. A few metres can make the difference between a tent blowing away and being buried and secure.* (1974)

RIGHT *Flying low over a lonely tent guarded by two dog teams. At every camp-site the layout is identical. The dogs are tethered so they can't quite reach each other and the tent sits between the two 'L's of the dog spans. The drifts around the camp indicate that the wind has been blowing fairly hard for some time. (1974)*

In 1936 the expedition geologist, Launcelot Fleming, found fossils in the stratified mountain behind this camp. It is now known as Fossil Bluff and gave its name to the four-man glaciological base set up at its foot.

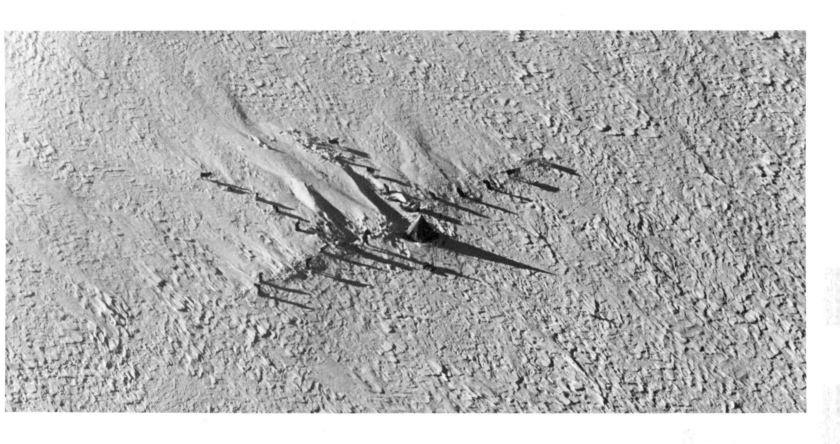

RIGHT *This camp was on a snow dome at the crest of the plateau, at about 2200 metres. Because of the weather, four men had to stay here twenty-two days in order to complete a four-day work programme. Here the tents are well drifted in after three days of incredible winds – up to an estimated maximum of 90 knots.* (1974)

Fortunately, it is rarely windy when temperatures are really low. Here it was −43°C and a gentle breeze is carrying the water vapour from the Primus fumes away from the peak of the tent. Great care has to be taken to keep the ventilator clear of frost crystals as an unventilated tent can easily asphyxiate the inmates. (1974)

RIGHT *This view of the Ellsworth Mountains includes the highest mountain on the Antarctic Continent, Vinson Massif, over 5100 metres. Christmas Day had been two days earlier and the field party had celebrated with a lie-in. But as the sun never sets at this time of year and they had twelve-hour watches they couldn't tell which day it was when they woke up.* (1979)

In windless, whiteout conditions the moisture in the air settles out as hoar-frost. Unlike snow, it cannot be heard falling and provides terrible running surfaces, like coarse desert sand. This scene was taken at 2000 metres where hoar-frost completely buried a tent set up as a weather station in three months. (1946)

This camp (ABOVE RIGHT) was pitched at the foot of a rock buttress overlooking George VI Ice Shelf for some survey work. Wind kept the two surveyors in the tent for fourteen days and when they emerged everything was buried in snow (BELOW RIGHT). Their fuel had run perilously low and they had even started trying to prime the stove with rum. (1973)

LEFT *In 1947 a four-man party from Hope Bay sledged 440 miles to a Christmas Day rendezvous with a group from Stonington Island. When they met, the Hope Bay party's rations were reduced to seven days' food, a bottle of rum and ten cigars and they would probably not have survived if the meeting had not gone as planned.*

George VI Ice Shelf sits over a deep sea channel. A small crack was found near the middle of the shelf-ice and a hole was chipped through to the sea allowing water temperatures and salinities to be measured down to depths of 370 metres. The results were used to help assess how water interacts with its permanent ice covering. (1974)

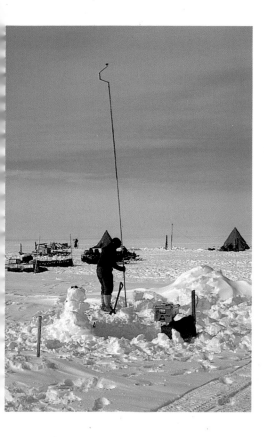

The laundry hanging round the tent is in fact a row of polythene bags filled with melted snow samples taken from the cores. (1976)

ABOVE *One of the glaciologist's jobs is to extract snow samples from depth and ship them north to be analyzed. The driller out of sight in a pit is helped by an assistant on the surface who holds the drill each time it comes up for the removal of a core. (1976)*

BELOW *This 2-metre pit has been dug to extract snow samples and the sides of the pit have been marked to show the obvious seasonal layering in the snow. Each layer represents a year's snowfall, so by counting downwards it is possible to put a date on any particular sample layer.*

ABOVE RIGHT *Cores like these were extracted from a 10-metre hole at the bottom of the pit. Uncontaminated samples are cut out of the cores, melted and poured into polythene bottles. These are carefully cooled and then refrozen and shipped to Denmark (BELOW RIGHT). Analysis of these samples tells us something of the temperature in the area at the time each sample was laid down. (1975)*

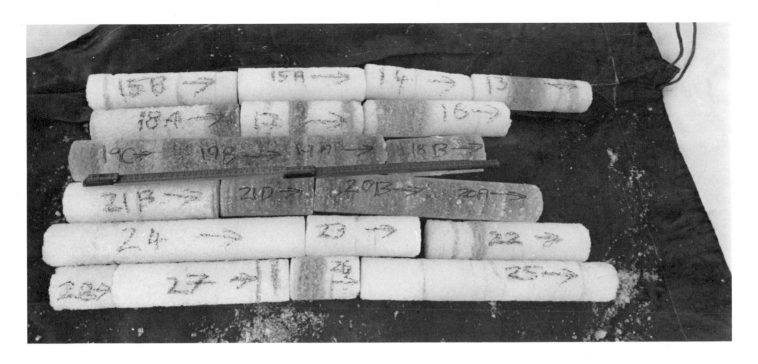

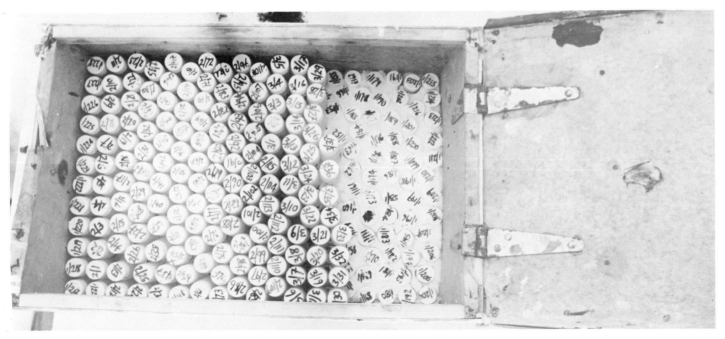

RIGHT *In the late 1950s an aircraft touched down while her altimeter was reading 1000 metres, thus leading to the important discovery that certain radio waves can penetrate ice. Sophisticated instruments have now been developed and it has been possible to map the entire sub-ice landscape of the Antarctic. This is a prototype instrument being tested in 1974.*

LEFT *Another common glaciological task is using traditional land-survey measurements to determine how ice flows and deforms. Here a theodolite is set up near the edge of the shelf-ice, where the ice has started floating after descending the heavily-crevassed Bertram Glacier. (1975)*

BELOW *In 1947 navigating on a reconnaissance survey involved using known compass courses and measuring distances by bicycle wheel. It was always a problem identifying mountain features as they tended to change shape hour by hour as one passed.*

A well-organized tent should be very warm and comfortable whatever is happening outside. When properly pitched, with 150 mm between the layers, a double-skinned tent can easily be kept warm with a Primus or pressure lamp, and socks and other small items can be hung in the peak to dry. For Jonathan Walton everything is within reach: the wireless, the cooking stove and the pressure lamp. Cooking is quick and the food easily, but not too easily, digested. (1975)

Dampness is what makes clothing cold which is why such emphasis is placed on keeping things absolutely dry. Here a party is drying out kit while waiting to move on – it is summer and far better to travel by the midnight sun when surfaces are frozen. (1945)

Even on a day when the wind is relatively gentle, it is not wise to linger outside for long. In gale conditions the near tent might just be visible and opening the sleeve only a fraction to look outside will cover everything inside with snow. Journeys outside are limited to bare essentials which get very cold in the process. (1975)

Sometimes ice crystals in the air reflect sunlight to
create wonderful effects. Here a prominent halo has
formed around the sun in rainbow colours, with bright
patches (mock suns) at the 9, 12 and 3 o'clock
positions. (1975)

In pressure ice the ice becomes heavily deformed, cracks occur and melt pools appear on the surface. Here the salinity of one such pool is about to be measured – the men are roped up in case the ice cracks still further. (1974)

Although the Antarctic Continent can't support wildlife, individuals do sometimes stray surprising distances inland. This penguin walked into camp 100 miles from the nearest sea and was returned by air in due course. (1974)

NAME: *RASMUS*   NO: F 5018/62.   DOG/~~BITCH~~   BORN: 1-4-62

BROTHER OF. LOLA. LOTUS. TUXEN. ARCHIE.

Father: *DART*.   No: Mother: *ROO*   No.: D/3170/60

Markings to be entered at age 12 months

Medical History: Dewormed 9.5.66.
Developed limp on N.E. Palmerland trip '66 '67. No outward symptoms.
A supturating wound on the front left leg in September 1967 treated by 4 intramuscular injections of penicillin

BADLY HEALED WOUND IN RT FR. LEG - CUT AGAIN & RE-STITCHED BY A.A.B. HEALING NICELY. '68 RAB. VAT.
SPLIT PAD IN RT FR. HEALED.   JD   WT. JAN 69 107 lbs

Characters:

GOOD:
Works well with brother Tuxen.

good worker.
Will work only when absolutely necessary.

Works a little more frequently, but mustn't be allowed to slack   JD   as before

BAD:
More excitable + weaker of pair.

Escape-artist!
Forever taking "tea breaks" on the run. Escapism finally prohibited by ingenious shackling.   '87.

as above lengthy marine with R 68 (Feb) keeping   JD   68 (Feb)

Living at close quarters in a small base in the field can lead to personality clashes however carefully base members are chosen. The presence of an old husky often helps to defuse situations and the one featured here, Rasmus, lived his last days at Fossil Bluff.

During the time that huskies were used for all journeys in Antarctica careful records were kept for each one noting their medical history, performance and good and bad habits. (1974)

In the Air

'SLEDGE WHISKY, SLEDGE WHISKY, this is UP-FAQ. Do you read?'

'AQ. This is Sledge Whisky. I read you. Long time no see. Thought that we had been forgotten.'

'AQ to Whisky. Sorry about that, but you are a long way away. What is your weather like?'

'Whisky to AQ. Dingle here – no cloud, no wind. Perfect landing conditions. Are you coming to get us?'

'AQ. Roger to that. At present we are about six miles short of Fossil Bluff at 1800 metres and will be on our way to you as soon as we have fuelled.'

A conversation like that must have started a very memorable few days flying in the late summer of 1979. Whisky was the call sign for a field party of four men and four skidoos camping some 500 miles south of the base at Fossil Bluff where the aircraft planned to refuel. They had been in the field for 46 days doing glaciological work near the Ellsworth Mountains, the highest mountain range in the Antarctic. For the first 38 days it had not been possible to make wireless contact with base and since then contact had been very erratic. The party still had food supplies and could have sledged out on their own in an emergency but it was a relief to know that they would be lifted out. The aircraft AQ and her sister AR were about to land at Fossil Bluff with a load of food and fuel having just been held up by ten days bad weather at the Rothera Point base.

Unfortunately the weather didn't clear for long. The two planes flew down to the Ellsworths and lifted the four men out but on the way back the weather was obviously closing in from the north so the pilots put the planes down in the middle of nowhere. It was two days before the wind blew itself out and the clouds cleared but when the break came they dug out the camp and the planes were soon airborne.

Once back at Fossil Bluff the planes dropped the field party, refuelled and returned 150 miles to Rothera Point. Fossil Bluff now had ten inhabitants rather than the four it was designed for, but this would provide an opportunity to get through the chores and the backlog of maintenance work. But after only four hours back in civilization another conversation over the air put Sledge Whisky in the field again. Two years before this party had planted tall aluminium poles on the Bach Ice Shelf to record ice movement and they needed to measure the new positions of these if the earlier work was not to be wasted. The wireless conversation went something like this:

'AQ calling Fossil Bluff. Does Sledge Whisky still want to go down to the Bach Ice Shelf? How does the weather look to the south-west? Is it good enough for a try?'

'Fossil Bluff to AQ. Yes. How long before you are with us?'

'AQ to Fossil Bluff. We are flying south and over Cape Jeremy. Give us 45 minutes.'

'Fossil Bluff to AQ. OK. We will be ready to load up as soon as you have refuelled.'

So, having just spent six weeks in the field and after only a few hours at Fossil Bluff, Sledge Whisky was removed for another two-week field trip.

This sort of operation is typical of aircraft work down south which is totally ruled by the weather. Two weeks of frustration at base may be succeeded by 72 hours of frenzied activity using all 24 hours of daylight before the next weather system moves in. Here a good day was taken advantage of to collect four men and their equipment from the field and then plans were changed again when there was a chance to put the party back into the field at very short notice. The planes will have done over 8000 miles of flying in three days.

Forty-five years earlier the story would have been very different. Aircraft are now more rugged and reliable and are designed to stand out without coming to any harm. The petrol-driven piston engines of earlier years were hard to start in cold weather and needed more servicing than the turbo-prop engines on modern aircraft. Now, planes do not have to be carried south as deck cargo as

PREVIOUS PAGE *Incoming aircraft nearly always make a low pass over an established camp in order to gain a sense of scale and assess the snow surface. The arrival of the aircraft means news, gossip, some fresh food, perhaps even a can of beer. Best of all, in this case it meant letters from home. (1979)*

they have the range to fly in independently and they are also powerful enough to compete with the gale-force winds that made earlier flying so hazardous.

When the earliest photographs here were taken pilots wore leather flying helmets, sat in open cockpits and flew by intuition with no aids apart from a magnetic compass. Now automatic pilots can do almost anything except land an aircraft or make judgements about surface conditions. But the apparent informality that surrounds flying today masks the lessons learnt from years of experience in Antarctic conditions. A flurry of snow can turn a perfect landing strip into a shadowless whiteout in a matter of moments, while a mechanical failure or a misjudged snow surface can transform an afternoon's outing into a situation of disaster.

ABOVE *This is the start of a very ambitious field trip from Stonington Island in 1946. It was a joint British/American venture and it was planned that there would be air support once the party had reached an area where it was safe for the aircraft to land (the two American support aircraft can be seen here). In the event, excessive loads and appalling sea-ice conditions forced a hurried retreat. (1946)*

RIGHT *The thin cloud moving in from the left is an unwelcome sight. Though a base airstrip will have the ability to talk a pilot down in poor visibility, this is not possible when the plane is landing in the field. Pilots will not usually fly to the field unless they know that the weather where they will land is clear – they prefer to wait for the perfect conditions of a 'dingle' day when there is virtually no cloud and to fly round the clock.* (1979)

LEFT *This is a very ominous sight for a pilot who would prefer not to be airborne in these conditions. On this occasion the plane was carrying a field party that would be put down some 440 miles further south where the weather was reported to be good. The plane will put down and wait for the weather to settle before returning. Underneath the cloud layer it would be overcast with little shadow.* (1979)

*In 1934 there was not much choice of aircraft for an
expedition with a limited budget. This all-wood
Fox Moth had an open cockpit for the pilot but the
passengers were in a closed cabin. Fitted with floats she
had a range of about 250 miles at 90 knots and was
very useful for reconnaissance. When at base, by using
a wire rope and a winch she could be taken out of the
hangar and launched by two men. Standing on a float
to swing the propeller to start the engine was a
precarious business. (1936)*

The pilot of a float plane had very bad forward visibility until the moment of take-off and he had to know that there was a clear stretch of water ahead, without even the smallest pieces of ice (which would do great damage to the floats), before he could start the take-off run. When under tow one person sat on a float fending off ice (and even on one occasion a whale) with his feet and the other float followed in the motor boat's wake. Once the aircraft was in the take-off position the boat would steer down the runway to create a wash as a float plane has great difficulty taking off from dead calm water. On a long flight there was always the risk that the landing area would have drifted over with ice again because of currents in the water, or a change in the wind. (1936)

LEFT *For obvious reasons, two aircraft are much safer and more productive than one. Here two De Havilland Twin Otter aircraft are flying in convoy which allows the passengers to obtain some unusual views of the 'other' plane. These aircraft spend March to October in Canada, flying the long return trip the length of the Americas each season. (1974)*

BELOW *Here the Twin Otters (or Twotters for short) have dropped a full field unit off and are warming up to head back to base to tackle the next task. Planes can fly almost continuously save for refuelling stops – it is humans that are the limiting factor and it has recently been accepted that two aircraft can be used much more efficiently if there are three pilots available to fly them. Without the skill of experienced pilots, field operations would be much less productive. (1979)*

LEFT *At the Debenham Islands in the spring of 1936 the sea-ice was relatively smooth and the Fox Moth could use skis instead of floats. As a result, the plane's performance and take-off weight improved and it was possible to carry 300 kilogrammes of cargo on a round trip of 250 miles. The eight boxes of field rations shown here are equivalent to about twenty days' food for three men and twenty-one dogs and will be dropped ahead of the sledge party they are intended for. This pilot developed his own technique for landing blind – he threw out a weighted flag which would stick into the snow surface and he would then fly low over it and get a fair idea of the wind direction, the scale of the sastrugi (snow-ridges) and general surface conditions.*

ABOVE RIGHT *Here the sastrugi are quite small and are soft enough to be broken down by the plane's skis, but after a long blow they can be half a metre or more in height and very hard. Without a person or object of known size on the ground which the pilot can use to gauge surface features it is impossible for him to estimate the scale of what he is seeing. Sastrugi can easily be mistaken for heavy crevassing if seen from the right height and vice versa. (1936)*

BELOW RIGHT *This lightweight monoplane was brought down by Trepassey as deck cargo in 1947 and was a civilian version of the Auster reconnaissance aircraft used in the services. Fitted with skis and long-range fuel tanks she could remain airborne for $7\frac{1}{2}$ hours and still carry a useful load. With a top speed of around 90 knots she had difficulty in flying in the strong winds that develop without warning from the plateau and this ultimately resulted in her loss. Eight hours after this photograph was taken she had turned on her nose when returning from a reconnaissance flight and had force-landed on the sea-ice 50 miles from base. The crew started to walk home using the long-range tank as a sledge but were rescued by air seven days later. (1946)*

ABOVE *At the beginning of each season in recent years a number of men have been dropped by ship about 190 miles north of Rothera base. The ice further south has been too thick for the ship so the party has been flown the rest of the way – and thence to their respective field camps. The route takes the planes through the narrow Lemaire Channel – the route for ships too in ice-free conditions. (1978)*

RIGHT *During the summer months Fossil Bluff becomes a busy airport with a constant traffic of planes to be loaded, unloaded, refuelled or serviced. Here a field party and their equipment are being loaded into one of the Twin Otters after a long and successful summer season for return to Adelaide base. (1975)*

LEFT *An Otter can only carry 1000 kilogrammes with full fuel tanks but with half-empty tanks the plane can be packed solid. (1975)*

RIGHT *Here the Otters are flying together again. The landing ski arrangement shows up well – if the planes take off on snow but need to land on a hard surface, the wheels can be lowered hydraulically to protrude through the skis. (1974)*

Planes can land and take off on snow as long as the surface is smooth. Although the take-off run could often go on for miles, these Otters are so powerful that they can take off in as little as 50 to 60 metres if they have no load. (1974)

RIGHT *Pilots and planes cannot operate without a dedicated team of aircraft engineers who are prepared to do most of their work in far from perfect conditions. They must also have excellent circulation in their fingers – it is very uncomfortable working with fuel-covered hands in −20°C. (1974)*

The pilot has to be able to tell what the snow surface is like from the air. If it is smooth and rock-hard like this the plane will slip all over the place. If the surface is covered with sastrugi he must estimate whether the skis can cut through them or if they will send the nose wheel through the fuselage. The wrong decision could write off a plane worth £600,000. (1975)

This soft snow surface presented no problems but a misjudgement about its depth could have meant several hours hard digging. This photograph was taken on Charcot Island where a two-man team were being left to take a latitude and longitude fix. As a result of their measurements, this 30-miles-square island was 'moved' by almost 19 miles. (1975)

This 1947-vintage helicopter was attached to the US Navy icebreaker Burton Island. *She visited the base at Stonington Island one breakfast time and hovered over the puppy pen while those inside took photographs – it was the first helicopter many of the base-members had ever seen. (1947)*

Helicopters are very fuel-thirsty and make heavy demands on maintenance crews but they come into their own for landing small parties in outlandish places, such as survey parties on mountain peaks. Here a single drum of fuel was being landed to a field party by a helicopter from HMS Endurance – she probably used a drum of fuel in the process. (1976)

The four scientists on Bird Island, South Georgia, were evacuated in 1982 when the Falkland Islands were invaded. Here they are being landed on HMS Antelope.

Wildlife

WILDLIFE IN THE ANTARCTIC depends on the sea. The extreme cold and penetrating winds on the continent itself have resulted in an uninhabitable, ice-covered desert where all moisture is frozen and nothing grows. Paradoxically, however, the very same conditions also generate ocean currents that are teeming with life.

Antarctic waters have a special character. This is partly because glaciers add nutrient minerals as they melt and dilute the saltiness of the sea, and partly because floating ice keeps the temperature cold and constant – the colder water is, the more lifegiving air stays in solution. In consequence, one-fifth of the world's marine life is able to thrive in the South Polar Ocean.

The basis of all Antarctic wildlife is plankton – minute plants drifting in the ocean currents and multiplying in the long daylight hours of summer. They convert the sun's energy into fodder for krill – tiny eight-legged creatures scarcely 60 millimetres long which drift in swarms totalling millions of tonnes. Krill dominates the complex food chains which support all Antarctic wildlife from the great whales and elephant seals to the small Wilson's petrels and the universal predators, the brown skuas.

Albatrosses, seals, penguins, petrels, indeed all forms of Antarctic wildlife may be seen anywhere between the Antarctic Convergence and the coasts of the continent, especially in winter when they range the ocean following food supplies. As you travel south the first Antarctic wildlife appears miles from land. Albatrosses and pintado petrels follow the ship or glide among the wavetops alongside. As you cross the line of the Convergence the sea temperature drops 3°C and everyone puts on warmer sweaters. The colour of the sea may also change, for if the microscopic marine creatures of the Antarctic drift over the boundary they die and float to the surface, sometimes attracting spectacular concentrations of petrels.

PREVIOUS PAGE *King penguins are seldom still or silent and seem to enjoy walking.* (1981)

Once in the zone of drifting icebergs penguins appear beside the ship 'porpoising' rhythmically as they leap out of the water to breathe. Further south still small parties of penguins and seals rest on ice-floes and watch the ship as it threads its way through the leads in the ice-pack. The really large colonies are on the fast ice or on the beaches of the Peninsula and the islands.

It is at such places that the birds and seals of the Antarctic must come ashore in the summer to mate and rear their young. They are warm-blooded and like man can adapt to the worst extremes of cold and wind, as long as they stay within reach of the sea and their food supplies. Suitable areas on the fringes of the Antarctic or on the Antarctic islands are few and far between and the best places attract astonishing concentrations of wildlife.

One such area is South Georgia. Two-thirds of the island is covered by glaciers but on its shores or on the offshore islets like Bird Island there are beaches and nesting sites in abundance. Moreover, by some trick of the ocean currents and the contours of the sea bed the waters round South Georgia are unusually productive of marine life, especially krill. Tiny Bird Island shares these advantages. Sealers seldom found its landing place, defended by stormy seas, and it remains free from rats or any other imported predator. As a result, it is an undisturbed microcosm of Antarctic wildlife and has been chosen by the British Antarctic Survey as a base for biological fieldwork.

On Bird Island, as everywhere throughout the Antarctic, the most striking characteristic of the animals and birds, apart from their sheer numbers, is that they show no fear of man. A fearless visitor can walk close among them. As with animals the world over, the facial expression of a seal or the behaviour of a penguin will often seem to stem from human needs and emotions. Sometimes the parallel is appropriate. An appealing look from a 160-kilogramme baby elephant seal may well be because it likes being scratched in those places its flippers cannot reach. Despite their lack of fear, however, Antarctic creatures are not in any sense tame and should be approached with respect. Young bull fur seals are always seeking to exercise those aggressive skills which may make them beachmasters of their own harems next year. It is essential at all times to carry a stout stick or 'bodger' to prod them in the chest if they rise up in challenge – this will keep them at a distance.

Albatrosses and giant petrels on the nest will not run away but they are big and may suddenly peck sharply. With practice they can be picked up to be ringed or weighed, or in order to take a blood sample. It is even possible to intercept parent albatrosses who have just returned from a trip to sea. If the timing is right they will regurgitate the krill or squid they were bringing back to feed the chicks into a plastic bag instead of into their offspring's bill. The evil-smelling ration is then borne away for analysis. The technique is borrowed from the sheathbills. Using their wits in this way these crafty scavengers win extra nourishment for their own young.

Such fieldwork is part of a continuing programme started in the fifties. It is only by long-term studies of this kind that the impact of commercial and tourist interests on each species can be watched and ways found to avoid undue disturbance of the web of indigenous wildlife.

Throughout any season the variety and interest of life on Bird Island is inexhaustible. Elephant seals come ashore in October to breed on stony beaches and fur seals follow in large numbers with the occasional Weddell or leopard seal. Before long there are pups everywhere, round and under the base hut and exploring up into the tussock meadows above. On level areas great wandering albatrosses are spreading their wingspans to over three metres in courtship displays round the nests. These are well spaced out to leave runways for their rather clumsy landings. Mollymawks and giant petrels choose higher terraces from which they can take off more easily over the sea. While they are incubating, small petrels hide in rocky crevices or burrows among the clumps of tussock grass during the day, appearing at night to change over with their mates and to feed on the phosphorescent plankton which rises to the surface of the sea.

Gentoo and chinstrap penguins build nests of stones but the quaint macaroni penguins breed on steep rock slopes covered by their own guano. One can become accustomed to the halitosis of bull seals or the evil-smelling oil ejected by giant petrels but never to the pungency of guano. Mercifully, high winds bring constant fresh air to most of the island!

The pictures that follow are a representative cross-section of Antarctic wildlife. By good luck and being in the right place at the right time all these birds and animals were taken near one of their favoured breeding places. For many of the creatures this was around Bird Island but some, for example the Adelie penguins and the crab-eater seals, were photographed far south among the ice-floes.

Even Bird Island is not a sanctuary without problems. The natural increase in the number of fur seals is causing them to encroach on the tussock meadows and their bird population. Out at sea the whale population is still endangered and thousands of tonnes of krill are being harvested and sold in Japanese supermarkets. The impact of man has far-reaching effects.

Antarctic wildlife is uniquely adapted to survive in the worst climate in the world and so far has proved resilient in the face of man's excesses. If the growing knowledge about these creatures is applied with wisdom there is at least a hope that they and their habitat will be preserved for future generations.

BELOW *There are about 30,000 birds in this king penguin rookery at St Andrew's Bay on South Georgia, and there are rookeries larger than this. (1981)*

RIGHT *King penguins make no nest but settle their egg on top of their feet where it is held by a fold of skin. With luck a pair raises two chicks every three years and a rookery will usually contain two age groups, the younger one, as shown here, still being fed by their parents. It is midwinter and the chicks need their brown furry coats. (1981)*

Like most birds, king penguins have a large vocabulary of elegant gestures with head and neck. (1981)

LEFT *Penguins fly underwater propelled by the flipper-like wings – feet and tail serve chiefly for steering. They can swim at 20 knots and can leap out of the water to land on their feet on rocks or ice-floes. On the surface they are much slower. This is an Adelie penguin. (1945)*

LEFT *Adelie penguins diving. All penguins dive well and king penguins carrying depth recorders have been found to dive to a depth of over 100 metres. (1973)*

RIGHT *Crab-eater seals really feed on krill and can live wherever there is ice on which they can haul out and breed. They are found in small parties, never in large colonies, and so did not suffer from sealers – but they have always been a convenient source of dog food. (1936)*

ABOVE *This typical 'mank' weather does not stop fur seal pups from exploring. Several of them are marked with paint for regular checks on weight. By Christmas (midsummer) they become too big to handle. The lone elephant bull lingering on the beach to moult is about three metres long. The white birds are sheathbills. (1980)*

FAR RIGHT *Bull fur seals grow as big as a farm cow with the teeth of an Alsatian dog and the manners of a football hooligan. (1983)*

RIGHT *Like most other seals, except fur seals and sea lions, Weddell seals appear slow and clumsy on land. This one was taken on the beach by Rothera base. (1976)*

LEFT AND BELOW *Fur seal pups and young bulls wander quite high up into the tussock grass behind the beaches on Bird Island. What looks like a charming family group* (LEFT) *is in fact a chance meeting. The cow and its pup belong but not the young ruffian on the right.* (1981, 1982)

ABOVE *Weddell seals are named after James Weddell who discovered both them and the sea that bears his name in 1823. These seals usually breed in small colonies on or near the Antarctic Continent but in winter they go under the ice where it is warmer. (1935)*

Elephant seal yearlings are about the same size as bull fur seals and tend to get mistaken for their rivals and rather knocked about. (1980)

Bull elephant seal roaring – the proboscis is inflated to increase resonance. (1981)

ABOVE *A bull elephant seal in repose. (1982)*

RIGHT *Leopard seals breed in inaccessible places among the ice-pack, do not form colonies and may turn up anywhere in the Antarctic to ambush young seals or penguins. Note the formidable teeth. (1980)*

LEFT *The blue-eyed shag nests near the sea on the Antarctic Peninsula or on the islands further north. They wear a yellow knob over the bill when breeding. (1981)*

BELOW *Northern giant petrels nesting on Bird Island. These birds are usually seen scavenging on the beaches and are referred to as 'stinkers' because they eject foul-smelling oil if disturbed. (1981)*

ABOVE *Mollymawk is an affectionate collective name for the smaller kinds of albatross, but even so these are big birds with a two-metre wingspan. This pair are grey-headed albatrosses. (1982)*

LEFT *Mollymawk's nests are a compact cylinder 300 millimetres across with a hollow in the top where the chick sits waiting for food. (1981)*

ABOVE LEFT *The light-mantled sooty albatross, perhaps the bird of the* Ancient Mariner. *These birds range right round the polar ocean and go very far south. They breed in small groups on terraces near the sea. (1982)*

About 700 fur seal pups were born on this beach on Bird Island in four weeks in 1981. The gantry, which keeps observers clear, is for studying seal behaviour – notes are taken in ten-minute periods, four times an hour, seven hours a day. (1980)

BELOW *Ringing a great wandering albatross. Permits to ring or band birds are only given to those who have learned how to hold them so that they don't struggle. Tucking the neck between your legs is traditional, but with experience you can talk some nesting birds into letting you lift out a leg, or even an egg, for inspection.* (1982)

The sea round South Georgia is unusually clean and free from pollution, but this king penguin turned up black with oil. He became a great pet (known as George) but eventually another lone king came ashore and the two went off together. (1981)

LEFT *Mollymawk chicks submit to being lifted from nest to weighing machine and back again with patient equanimity. One chick ceased to gain weight while its mother carried a radio transmitter recording her time in the air and on the sea, but resumed its usual rapid growth when the radio was attached in such a way that it did not interfere with her fishing.* (1980)

RIGHT *Great wandering albatrosses display before pairing, which is for a lifetime of up to thirty years, and also before nesting. The birds dance round each other with outstretched wings, or raise their bills uttering ecstatic, low-pitched cries. These are the largest flying sea-birds in the world.* LEFT *Wanderer eggs are laid in December and hatch about eleven weeks later. The tubular nostrils common to all albatrosses and also to petrels show well on the parent here.* BELOW LEFT *Wanderer parents continue to take turns on the nest until the chick is six weeks old. Then both will bring back food until the nestling is nine months old and ready to fly. They breed only every second year. Birds are dark all over when they take their first flight but this turns to delicate pencilling at successive moults and the oldest birds are white with only the wingtips dark. (1982)*

There are more Adelie penguins
than there are of any other species.
They live far south and are plump,
fluffy and well-feathered round the
beaks to keep out the cold. They
can walk almost as fast as a man
and many trek forty miles from the
sea to find secure ice and stones for
nest-building. (1974)

RIGHT *Chinstrap penguins are similar to Adelies but they have a pugnacious character to go with their guardsman's chinstrap. Many more large colonies have been discovered recently. (1974)*

BELOW *This is a gentoo colony on Bird Island. The two birds in the foreground are chinstraps but most of those behind have the distinctive white cap that marks a gentoo. (1981)*

ABOVE *Apart from their white caps, gentoo penguins are also distinguished by the bright orange-yellow of their beaks and feet. The birds swimming further out are giant petrels.* (1982)

LEFT *Macaronis are quaint little penguins who nest in very dense colonies on rocky ledges close to the sea. Distinguished by their quiff of yellow feathers, they are tough and resilient and can bounce ashore out of ten-metre waves. There are about five million on the islands off South Georgia. (1974)*

ABOVE *There are about 200 birds in this picture, part of a king penguin crèche at St Andrew's Bay on South Georgia. (1981)*

One midnight at midsummer on Stonington Island the met man left the hut door open when he went outside to make his scheduled observations, leaving his three companions sleeping quietly. This Adelie penguin walked in while he was out and made a thorough and highly vocal inspection. After the chaos subsided George went on his way with a friendly wave. (1946)